Becoming

Magic

GENEVIEVE DAVIS

Disclaimer: The author bears no responsibility for any consequences resulting from the use of information provided in this book. Please use all information at your own risk. No part of this publication may be reproduced or transmitted in any form without the express permission of the author.

Becoming Magic

A Course in Manifesting an Exceptional Life

Book 1

Genevieve Davis

CONTENTS

1 IS THIS IT?

Have you always had a lurking feeling you were meant for better things? Are you depressed, do you feel unfulfilled, angry or bitter about how life has treated you? Do you resent the fact that other people seem to have endless success, luck and happiness while life kicks you in the teeth, over and over and over? Perhaps you feel you have some great talent, waiting to be discovered. Do you know you would be capable of so much more, if only you were given the opportunity? Do you go through life thinking *life was not supposed to be this way, I am worth more than this, why are my talents not recognized?* Or do you have a sense of longing, of searching for something you know not what? Do you feel unappreciated in your job, your family, perhaps even in your relationship? Do you feel that in some place, in another life, you would be shining like a diamond, rather than ignored and unnoticed as you are now: just another face in the crowd?

If you believe deep down that you are special, this is not some delusion; this reflects an underlying truth about you and the immensity of your true underlying power. At the moment, it's just obscured from view. In the way is garbage in the form of unhelpful beliefs, negative messages from the media and society, worry and negative thinking. It doesn't matter how old you are or what color you are; it doesn't matter how educated or intelligent you are; it doesn't matter if you are considered beautiful or ugly; it doesn't matter whether you were born into extreme poverty and are living in a wooden shack or mud hut. I put it to you that you are still perfect, divine, and *unbelievably* powerful. Somewhere, deep down, your greatness is sitting ... and waiting.

In the two small books of this course, you will rediscover that greatness and begin to reclaim your birth-right. You will begin to awaken from the sleep that you have been living in for most of your life. At first, you will imagine that creating your own reality is all about manifesting possessions, money, a new job, a new partner. It's true: you *will* learn to manifest particular material things. But you'll soon realize that getting more stuff is only the beginning and you will soon come to see how insignificant these things really are. Manifesting material possessions is great, but only because it is a stepping-stone to the next stage.

Something much more spectacular than material riches awaits you. You have an entire life of wonder to which to look forward. A life without fear, without hardship, without poverty is at your fingertips. Read these books, one at a time. Master this ability, thoroughly, completely and you will begin to live your life with a sense of aliveness, of expectation, and of sheer joy. You will work miracles. *You will be the miracle you are.*

At your core, you may already suspect this to be true. If there is greatness within you, you should feel a pang of recognition when you read this short book. You will not have to be convinced by what I say; instead, you will feel a wonderful sense of things ringing true for you. If reading this book feels less of a learning, and more of a remembering, a recognizing, then greatness is within you.

Welcome to book one of your course in Magic. For many of you, this book will not be your first dabble into the Magical foray. Some of you will be familiar with the Law of Attraction, Reality Creation, Positive Thinking and their like. Some of you will be Self-Help fans or Personal Development students. But still others will be new to this new and fascinating field of human thought and behavior.

It is my intention to lead you by the hand through a marvelous journey of wonder and adventure. This book lays the groundwork, while the one that follows offers concrete techniques and instructions for bringing wonderful things into your life. The plan is to build your knowledge slowly, gradually, building on what has gone before, moving on to more complex techniques only once the basics are mastered.

So many people fail with Magic and the Law of Attraction because they rush headlong into using techniques, trying to create enormous manifestations, making very simple but crucial mistakes.

When they are disappointed, they imagine they have been duped. The skeptics are right. This is all a load of scammy nonsense. And they give up, declaring *it just doesn't work.*

I am telling you that it *does work.* And *you can make it work.*

And in this short book, I hope to show you some of the reasons that it may not have worked for you so far, what you can do about it, and so turn you from one of the bitter, newly-skeptical failures, into a powerful creator, a sorcerer, a wizard.

Note that this book is not marketed. It has no advertising. You will have received it free or very cheaply. That it has fallen into your hands is through pure chance. You can choose to see that as a lucky or unlucky coincidence, or you can choose to see it as something more portentous.

Put away your rational mind, and *feel.* If you feel nothing when reading, put the book down, deem it a waste of time and move on. But if you feel an excited sense of belonging, of coming home, of *truth,* then keep reading. Does this seem exactly what you are looking for? Does the timing of your finding this book seem a little *too* perfect to be dismissed as mere coincidence? Do my words seem to speak to you? Do you feel excited at the very thought of this? Do not fight that feeling. *Keep reading.* I may be exactly what you have been searching for. Prepare to be amazed, for this book is like no other.

You may be about to have the best year of your life. Everything you have searched for, been waiting for, been looking for may be just about to fall into your lap. It has sought *you* out.

Because what I am talking about feels mysterious and often so confusing, I prefer not to tie it down with such definite terms as 'Law' of Attraction.

I prefer to talk of doing *Magic.*

2 MAGIC?
I DO HOPE YOU ARE JOKING!

That is what I would have said, five or ten years ago. I once despised all things New-Age, all these spiritual types and their airy-fairy views, their bad science and their irrational beliefs.

Why Magic? Well, what is the definition of something working, although you have no idea how it works? Something happening with no clear explanation of how it has come about? Causation of events, acquirement of possessions and impossibly serendipitous circumstances that confound and confuddle even an intelligent, educated person with a scientific background? You call that *Magic.* Call it *Law of Attraction* if you prefer, or *Reality*

Creation or *Deliberate Manifestation*. I prefer *Magic* because of the way that this does not seem to follow any set rules, although many are now attempting to describe what is going on in terms of scientific laws. So do not get hung up on the name used to describe what is going on: Law of Attraction, Reality Creation, Deliberate Manifestation or Magic – it is not important.

Ever since I was a child I had a sneaking feeling that there was supposed to be more than this, that there was supposed to be more *for me.* Through my teens and twenties I just *knew* greatness was coming to me. My amazing and wonderful life was going to start any moment. After all, I knew that I could do *anything,* and that during my life I probably would do *everything.* And I was in no hurry because I was young and felt immortal. I had *decades* left to start my magnificent life. But as my twenties turned to thirties, there was still no sign of this magnificent life. I had a few bad relationships, failed businesses and had got terribly into debt. It felt like I had been forgotten. I was destined for greatness, but my life was playing out in the most ordinary and mundane way.

As I turned forty, I began to feel that my magnificent years had been and gone. It was becoming too late, and I was too old to shine. The best of my years were behind me. There was nothing better to come. *This was as good as it was going to get!*

How had this happened? How had I managed to waste my potential so badly? How had I overridden my destiny in such a deleterious way?

Around ten years ago, I had fallen upon the School of New Thought, forerunners to today's Law of Attraction writers. I read *Think and Grow Rich* and was transfixed by Napoleon Hill's words, *Thoughts Become Things*. This little phrase rang around in my head day and night. I was entranced by the idea that just by changing my thoughts, I could change my entire life. If only I could think of something long and hard enough, and in the right way, it would come to me. I began to dabble with this way of thinking, just out of curiosity really, just to test it. I read everything I could find, from the greats such as Napoleon Hill, Charles Haanel, Wallace Wattles, Esther Hicks and Wayne Dyer, to all the bandwagon-jumpers, those with the hard-sell websites and impossible promises.

I followed different courses, different writers and gurus. I did countless visualizations, created vision boards and said my affirmations diligently.

But I encountered a snag, rather an overwhelming snag: I couldn't make it work. Any success I did have was sporadic, at best. Most of the time, nothing happened at all. Sometimes everything went catastrophically wrong, and I managed to manifest, not what I had asked for, *but the exact opposite!* I don't know why I ever kept going; blind faith and hope, I suppose. Any good scientist would have rejected the whole venture after seeing my pathetic results.

Until this point I had been blindly following the words of others, following their exact instructions and waiting for results. I followed Napoleon Hill's instruction to write down your desire and read it out three times a day, and I thought that would be enough. I cut out photos of lovely things and stuck them to a piece of MDF, thinking the cutting and the sticking had some sort of power over events in the world. It was only when I recognized, accepted and finally embraced that what I was doing was actually some kind of *Magic* that suddenly things began to fall into place.

Once I realized that the power came from within *me*, it was as if the light had suddenly been switched on.

Let me explain: think of a cartoon or child's film. An unsuspecting person picks up a magic wand, stolen from a wizard, waves it and says 'Abracadabra'. Some Magic occurs, a man turns into a frog or a chest of treasure appears. *This* is how I had been attempting to use Magic.

This is also exactly how most people attempt to use the Law of Attraction – as if it were something separate from them, something to be utilized, tapped into, picked up and put down. Thus they conscientiously follow the instructions of others, while failing to realize the importance of themselves as an active constituent in the process. The world does not respond to the waving of the wand, but *to the person doing the waving.* Some people do use Magic words, and some use paraphernalia such as wands, some use affirmations and vision boards with great success. *But the Magic itself always comes from the person doing the spell.* Two people could say the same words, follow the same instructions, wave the same wand, and get completely different results.

At some point, I began to 'look within'; I began to watch, to notice, to take notes, to become aware of what was going on *in me*, while all this was going on. I came to see that Magic is something you have to *become aware of within you.* Trying to do Magic by blindly following the words of others is like trying to taste a strawberry by reading about it.

And so, I began to loosen up on the strict adherence to someone else's 'rules'. I methodically began to notice the effect that *I had on the world.* I began to notice and become aware of my own power, my own enormous effect on the things around me; this effect had always been there but I had never noticed until now. And with that, my life turned around. All the things I had most desired, money, friends, a partner, mental stability, all started to come to me, *like Magic.* The more I noticed my own power, the more powerful I became. It was as if by becoming aware of my own Magic, that ability to do Magic increased. Instead of explaining fortuitous events away as coincidence, I saw everything as evidence of my own power ... and that power began to increase.

As a writer, I kept a detailed journal of notes, recording every last little thing that occurred. This little book is the result of those years of working with, struggling with and almost giving up over the so-called 'Law' of Attraction, or *Magic*, as I prefer to call it.

3 WHAT IS MAGIC?

I am not some sort of mystical moon child. I do not have a name like Unicorn Goddess, River Child, or Angel Blossom. I do not have a house full of crystals or pentagrams. I do not invoke spirits, goddesses or the like.

I make no judgment of those who like to use paraphernalia such as crystals and candles, vision boards or gratitude stones. I simply choose not to use them because such things make no sense to my understanding, they do not speak to me.

Some people use such paraphernalia with great success *because it allows them to get in touch with their own power and Magic.* And if having crystals and pentagrams and pictures of goddesses makes you *feel* Magic, if they get you in touch with that power within, if they get your magical juices flowing, *then they are completely and absolutely right for you.*

Magic does not belong to Wiccans, or any other sorts of 'witch'. It has nothing to do with devil worship or calling upon evil spirits. I do not call on any spirits whatsoever.

Magic is not for the seventh daughters of seventh daughters. It is not those descended from King Arthur or Aleister Crowley. Being Magic is not only for the educated, or the middle-classes. It is not even for the intelligent. There are many, many very successful people who have low intelligence and education. A simple, uncluttered mind can even be an asset when doing Magic.

If you live in a slum and never finished school, you can still do Magic; or you can be a Prince living in a palace. Magic is open to all.

I am not interested in anyone who talks of the 'true way' or the 'original way'. No one 'owns' the correct knowledge of how to do Magic. That sort of talk smacks of religious dogma. And there is *no* place for religious dogma in successful Magic.

Thinking you must follow someone else's dogma will obscure *your* own innate ability to do Magic yourself.

We do not need to look to a past time, or to go into a circle in the woods to do Magic. We can do Magic here, now, on the bus, on our smartphones, on our iPads, in the office, in the car. We do not need to become vegans, grow our own organic food, or campaign for social change.

Magic is not making things appear out of thin air (although with practice, this is pretty close to what can be achieved). It is a feeling. A sparkling aliveness. It is that energy of feeling you are capable of anything, in the flow, in the zone, on top of the world, *dancing with life.* In this dance, sometimes you lead and life swirls around you; at other times, life takes the lead, but always, you move with each other and respond to each other.

When you feel like this, when you are able to dance *with* life instead of reacting *to* life, instead of straining *against* it, *you are capable of anything!* It is when you are in this state that amazing things happen to you, consistently and reliably.

Magic is about walking around with so much charisma that strangers smile at you. It is having such a feeling of wondrous expectation that it is no surprise when desirable things just drop into your lap. And it is about *feeling special.* And feeling special is *not* limited to the super-rich, the super-famous or the super-clever.

Most people will only experience tiny glimpses of this state, perhaps just a few times in their lives. Some may not have created any Magic in years, decades even. Years of disappointment, negative messages and low moods (perhaps even bouts of depression) may have left you feeling hopeless, powerless and at the mercy of the world and its difficulties.

You are *not* an insignificant dot in an infinite universe. You are a hugely important, powerful creator. You are a wizard, a sorceress, a god.

If you're fed up with being made to feel inadequate, underprivileged and powerless by school, government and the media, if you always *knew* you were meant for bigger and better things, then it is time to turn your nose up at all of it and embrace your own Magic nature.

My intention is to waken the world to the Magic that is still very much alive, in the world and *in you*.

So, why this book? Why read *another* book on top of all the other hundreds out there?

If you are expecting me to reveal the technique that will allow you to manifest a million dollars by the weekend, you have come to the wrong person. I don't claim to have discovered the 'one weird trick' for mastering Magic, I have *not* found the 'hidden secret' to the Law of Attraction (because there *isn't* one). While reading this book, you won't just be told another wishful thinking fairy-tale, you won't be told how quick and simple this all is going to be.

You *will* be shown all the pitfalls, the mistakes and the things that stop Magic from working. And if you have any experience of trying and failing with Magic or the Law of Attraction, you will *recognize* these as mistakes you have made yourself.

There are lots of people offering advice as to why the Law of Attraction sometimes doesn't work. Everyone has a different reason for why manifestation is not working for you – perhaps you don't want it enough, you aren't clear enough in setting your intentions, you just aren't persistent enough, you aren't vigilant enough ... the list goes on.

Rather than asking you to take my word over theirs because I know better, I ask you to read my reasons, my words and decide for yourself whether they ring true for you. Do I answer all those questions you have wanted asked? Do I seem to make sense where no one else has? Do I seem to describe, not some hypothetical fantasy world, but *your experience?* I do not ask you to take anything I say as true. I invite you to test it all for yourself, not against what you *want* to be true, but *against your own experience.* I am hoping you will identify with a lot of what I am about to tell you. That is why you should listen to me.

But I must warn you. Contrary to what you may have been told elsewhere, this is very likely *not* going to be an easy process. There are a lot of other books telling you just what an easy process this is.

"All you need do are these very easy steps and everything will fall into your lap. And I will only tell you those six easy steps if you give me 3 monthly installments of $47.95"

This book is not one of them.

It seems to me that the easier a book tells you this process will be, the more that book will sell. The way to sell more books, especially if you don't know what you are talking about, is to make the process appear as easy and effortless as possible. *Be a millionaire by the weekend. One strange trick to manifest your soul mate.* The titles are compelling. But this doesn't make them truthful or realistic. These sorts of approaches remain very attractive, promising such huge rewards for little effort. They appear so simple that it's easy to fall for their charms. But don't let the supposed ease of a course or approach fool you into thinking it is therefore more effective.

Those that tell you that Magic or manifesting is an easy process are being disingenuous. It is true that for some people, everything 'clicks' first time and they get the hang of this reality creation in a snap. But to suggest that you will automatically be able to get the great results immediately is just not true for most people. The process of Mis very simple, that much is true. Does this mean it is easy? *No, a thousand times no!* For *most* people, probably more than 95%, this *will not be an easy process!*

Does that put you off? Do you now wish you had bought the 'six easy steps' course from that website? You know, the one that promised you would be a millionaire by the weekend?

Most Law of Attraction writers are intelligent, clever people who speak from the heart and who really seem to know what they are talking about, Esther Hicks, Wayne Dyer and Eckhart Tolle are three you should look up. But for every Esther or Eckhart, there are a dozen dodgy-looking websites which have done nothing more than jumped on the gravy train with no real knowledge or experience. It is these somewhat disingenuous writers that have caused the massive distrust in the Law of Attraction.

If all we had were the Esthers, the Waynes and the Eckharts, it is my belief that all of this would be taken a lot more seriously.

I am *not* writing a mass appeal book. I am attempting to cut through the misleading hyperbole and outlandish claims you are bombarded with online.

Here are my cards, laid out on the table:

I am selling this book very cheaply or free

I will tell you what I know, whether or not it turns out to be popular.

I do not have a long thin website with a big red headline at the top telling you 'this one weird trick will make you a millionaire', or 'single mom makes $2000 a day working from home'.

Whenever I do make any profit from these books, I give that profit away. (It always comes back to me!)

In this book, and its counterpart, *Doing Magic*, I don't create a fantasy vision of a future world which bears no relation to your own experience of life. I am not one who had instant and profoundly amazing success right off the bat. You should trust me because I *didn't* get it right first time. I didn't get it right second, third, fourth, fifth or sixth time either! I am one who has made mistake after mistake, readjusted, recorded the results and carried on! I am someone who has been where you are, experienced what you feel, had the same crappy results for years and years *and learned how to turn it around!*

I am telling you now, that I made a long, slow discovery of the rules of Magic.

If you are fed up with the 'one weird trick' brigade, with empty promises and expensive mistakes, you should continue to read.

If you are committed to reading, studying, applying yourself, taking notes and giving this the time that it needs, *I can show you the way to becoming Magic and creating a dream life.*

I can promise you only one thing: all the hard work will be worth it.

4 KEEP IT QUIET

I'm not going to suggest that you pass this book on to all your friends, tell your blog, and announce it to your Facebook page.

Not yet, anyway!

While I ask you to believe that Magic exists, I don't recommend you shout this belief from the rooftops. At least in the beginning, may I suggest that you *don't* tell people what you are doing? Far better to at least get some success under your belt before you announce to the world how you have achieved it.

I learned very quickly to stop telling people what I was doing. I just got fed up with having to argue that my sudden success was not down to fluke or luck or coincidence, but down to what I had been doing behind the scenes. To this day, even most of my family do not know what I am up to. Hence the writing behind a pen name, no website and an anonymous email address.

I'm not saying you necessarily need to be as furtive as I have been. But you should be aware that most people are very threatened by things they don't understand. If you tell all and sundry that you are doing Magic *before* you are successful, they *will* disagree with you, laugh at you, try and ridicule you and even try and bring you down. You could then become demoralized and doubting. Doubt is the enemy of Magic; you cannot risk tempting doubt.

Instead of telling your friends you are 'doing magic', *wait until they ask.* When they see the upturn in your life, they will want to know where it has come from. Quite possibly, they will ask you to teach *them* what you know. That is the point at which you can think about recommending this book to your friends!

5 HOW DOES THIS ALL FIT WITH A SCIENTIFIC WORLD-VIEW?

I think it is hilarious the way that some people will reject these books as unscientific. Others try hard to show how the Law of Attraction fits with quantum physics. That is all fine. I will be delighted if someone manages to show that Magic fits with science, but that will not validate its efficacy in any way.

Is Magic unscientific? *I don't care two hoots one way or the other.* I have no desire to make what I do fit with a scientific worldview. I do not give a flying fig whether it does or doesn't fit with quantum physics or Newton's laws. (Incidentally, did you know that quantum physics *does not* fit with

Newton's Laws?) It works. And it works, whether or not it fits with Science, Christianity, Judaism, or anything else.

These days, I don't bother defending myself or my views. I don't care if someone thinks this is all baloney. Those who seek to argue, prove me wrong or dismiss my views are less than irrelevant to me. They are to be pitied – they will never know the joy, the power of what I can do, *what you are about to do.*

Dear reader, let me assure you that what I am calling 'Magic' has taken me from fat, lonely, anxious, depressed and destitute, to living in a gorgeous house on the coast, with a younger boyfriend, an almost unmanageably busy social life, more money than I know what to do with and almost constant happiness. If any scientist wants to come and tell me that's all rubbish because it's unscientific, I'm just not interested.

Are my beautiful house, my lovely partner and all my friends going to puff into smoke because someone 'proves' to me that what I have been doing is unscientific? Am I going to stop doing what has brought me all these things because someone who doesn't even know me thinks they have a superior intellect and tries to show how wrong I am? I think not.

But how does it work?

Do you want to know the truth? *I don't know. That is precisely why I call it MAGIC!*

FOR THOSE PUT OFF BY ALL THIS SELFISHNESS AND MATERIALISM

If you think that using Magic is an indication of a selfish and materialistic nature, you are completely wrong. Do you know just how much *good* you can do when you have more money, time and freedom than you know what to do with? I give a large proportion of my income away every month. I do loads of charity and voluntary work, because I have the money and the freedom to do so. If I get good service in a coffee shop, I leave a $50 tip. If I hear that a local child needs a special operation their parents cannot afford, I arrange for money to be sent, anonymously. I do 100% more good as a rich person than I ever did as a poor person!

You may be interested to know that these books were only written in order to raise money for a particular worthy cause. I have vowed never to make a penny for myself from teaching Magic to others. I make enough money from other sources not to have to do that. I suppose it's a strange superstition of mine, but I feel that if I make money from teaching other people how to make money, I am being dishonest. There is a sort of conflict of interests within me which doesn't sit well on my conscience. So rest assured, if you spent a few pennies on this book, your money has not gone to line my pocket.

6 THE STEPS TO ACHIEVING ANYTHING

1. ASK

2. RECEIVE

Yes, that's it.

'Yeah right,' you say, 'I ask for things all the time, but I hardly ever receive them.'

So why doesn't it work?

The main thrust of this little book is to prepare you for the process of asking and receiving so that it works! If there is one 'secret', one 'trick', one underlying principle that I want to get across to you, it is this: *If you don't get the receiving part right, your asking is going to achieve precisely nothing.* Because here's the kicker: Successfully manifesting is less about asking for things, less about *doing* Magic and almost entirely about *receiving*, in other words, *becoming, allowing* and *being* Magic.

This is the piece of knowledge that will turn your manifestation attempts from floundering accidents into inspired fantasies. It is this that will turn this process from difficult and confusing to feeling like one big, fun game. Get this right and you will see miracles appear in your life.

7 LEARN HOW YOU GET IT WRONG SO THAT YOU CAN GET IT RIGHT

Let's begin with our magical preparations. The first stage is to impart a little understanding and knowledge. No one should ever take anything on faith alone which is why I want to spend a little while explaining exactly why things may have gone wrong for you in previous attempts.

I'm now going to say something which verges on sacrilege in Law of Attraction circles. This may seem to fly in the face of all you have heard before from people such as Napoleon Hill, *The Secret* and others.

I don't say this to be controversial, but only because I believe it is right.

Forget all about 'thoughts become things'

You probably have heard from every book out there that we need to take our minds *off* what we don't want and *onto* what we do want, so that the way to manifest your desires is to think about them as often as possible. Thoughts become things; we create our world with our thoughts, and so on.

In Napoleon Hill's classic, *Think and Grow Rich,* he suggests you write your goal on a piece of paper and recite the words several times a day. Other writers suggest that you must develop focus and concentration in order to manifest your desires. Lack of clarity of thought is often cited as one of the main reasons that desires fail to manifest. So you may have been advised to think about your goal as often as possible, to read placards to yourself, to visualize, do affirmations, to flood your mind with ideas about the goal.

I am telling you that's all **wrong.**

Before you throw this book away in disgust, let me ask you some questions which should prove to you that I am making sense…

How many times have you tried visualizing, thinking constantly about your desire, and yet have nothing materialize.

How many times have you tried visualizing, thinking constantly about your desire only to *have the opposite appear in your life?*

How many times have you expected a particular event to turn out brilliantly, visualized it in perfect, intricate detail, only to *have it turn out completely differently?*

Have you also noticed that when you look forward to a wonderful event, with huge anticipation, having imagined every last detail, *it often disappoints?*

When bad things *do* happen, do they happen when you have been thinking about them, or do they appear to come along completely *out of the blue?*

We are told again and again that if we *expect* things to turn out badly, they *will.* I have lost count of how many times I have been told not to talk of worst-case scenarios because in doing so I will 'make them happen' and so court disaster. *Speak of the Devil and he will appear*, so the saying goes.

Just for a moment, I want you to forget about what you have been told, and forget about what is *supposed* to be true.

How many times has this actually happened to you? How many times have you expected the very worst, and then seen that same very worst case scenario appear in your life?

Once? Never?

Have you instead noticed that by expecting the worst, things almost *always turn out better than you expected?* I am willing to bet money that when you have expected things to turn out very badly you have often been pleasantly surprised by the actual outcome. Perhaps you went to a party in a really bad mood, not expecting to enjoy yourself at all, but ended up having a really good time. A presentation or meeting at work which you had worried about for weeks turns out to be a total success. Or you didn't want to watch a particular film, sure it was going to be a massive disappointment, only to find it was excellent. I also wager that when bad things have happened in your life, they have usually done so completely without warning and *not* at all because you have been thinking about them.

How can this ever be true? How can any of these things possibly happen if the Law of Attraction says you attract just what you think about, what you focus on?

These results would seem to suggest, contrary to all you have been told, that thinking about bad things makes good things happen, and thinking about good things makes bad things happen?

What on earth is going on?

If you have experienced these sorts of results, don't despair. Just because you haven't had any luck with 'thoughts become things' don't imagine the fault lies with you. Don't assume that everyone else is getting it right, and that you simply need to try harder, think harder, or concentrate more. My belief is that *most people get these sorts of 'anomalous' results.*

To explain this, let's consider another example - Have you ever found that the very thing you have been trying desperately to manifest for months, years even, miraculously appears just when you had stopped even thinking about it, perhaps forgotten all about it, perhaps even once you had stopped *wanting* it? This is *not* misfortune and this is *not* coincidence.

This happens because until that point you had actually kept the goal just out of reach by your constant attention to it. By applying 'thoughts become things', you prevented that goal from manifesting. It was only when you dropped your attention that it was able to come to you.

But why does this happen?

It's because, for almost all of us, when you think of something you really want *you really want it.* And here's something you need to burn into your brain: *Want is another word for lack.* Thoughts of wanting only attracts more wanting and more lack. By continually thinking about your goal, you are continually wanting, continually asking. This will act to 'freeze' things, keeping you in a state of constant state of waiting, wanting, anticipation and lack.

Wanting = Asking = Lack

I am not claiming there is no truth to *thoughts become things.* I just find it a very strange instruction to give to beginners. It is a strange instruction because it is not just discrete individual *thoughts* that become things, but rather the entire package, the entire person, the beliefs, tendencies, energy, confidence levels and *actions* that a person with those thoughts will tend to carry out.

For beginners, positive thoughts about goals and desires are often in conflict or opposition to these other aspects of that person.

Remember, there are two parts to the magical process: *asking* and *receiving*. When the disparity between our thoughts and the rest of our life is great, the action of thinking about a goal only serves to bring more sharply into focus just how much we want and lack that goal. So for most people, keeping their goal constantly in mind just keeps them stuck in the asking stage. This stops them ever being able to progress to the receiving stage, and so, they *never* receive what they are asking for.

If you do not stop asking for your desire, you'll never receive it.

45

I fully accept that there are some people who are able to use the principle of *thoughts become things* successfully from the very beginning, without having to study or experiment at all. In *Doing Magic* I outline one of the most effective techniques for manifesting anything and which is based on this very principle. But I certainly don't recommend that you start out by using it.

People who have a lot of success with *thoughts become things* are often those who already consider themselves to have full and happy lives. For example, a person who is already financially wealthy finds it very easy to focus on money without fear, or doubt or feelings of lack. A person attracts money, not just because they one day decide to think about a million dollars, but because *the type of person they are* means they tend to think rich thoughts naturally.

On the other hand, a person who has nothing *cannot usually imagine having money without simultaneously comparing it to how poor they really feel.*

I have met two or three people in my life who were immediately able to manifest a completely new life just by focusing clearly on the object of their desire.

I have a few theories about why some people are able to do this. Largely, I believe it is down to a sort of healthy naivety and a calm, uncluttered mind.

I have noticed that those who are able to use *thoughts become things* off the bat, are those who do not tend to question things, and who are very straightforward, well-balanced people, are naturally able to let go of thinking of their desires, and so move effortlessly to the second stage of the magical process.

If you (like me) have an active, questioning mind that just won't shut up with its incessant questioning, worrying and wondering, then *you are not one of these people!*

If you find it impossible to think of your desires without desperately *wanting* them, then *you are not one of these people!*

If you *haven't* had that sort of instant success yet (and the fact you're reading this book tells me you probably haven't) then *you are not one of these people!*

And if you *are* one of those incredibly lucky people born with the natural ability to do Magic, put this book down and get on with your wonderful life.

8 FROM DISAPPOINTMENT
TO DANGER

But now, I'm really going to shake things up. There is a frightening truth about using Magic: if you don't get it right, a lot *worse* can happen other than just not getting what you want.

You have probably heard about the 'magic of thinking big', that you can achieve *anything,* no matter how huge, if you set your mind to it. After all, Richard Branson and Donald Trump didn't get where they did by thinking small.

Why let society, parents and negative messages from the media keep you down? You are going to go straight in and go for the biggest, shiniest goal on your list. Nothing is going to stop you and you are going to keep going until you get it. After all, you deserve this huge, magnificent goal as much as anyone. Why *shouldn't* you go for it?

No reason whatsoever… just as long as you are used to thinking this big, and used to reaching massive goals, taking huge risks, doing scary things and achieving great successes. If this is all true then it is absolutely right that you go for your massive goal straight away.

But, if you are currently *not* living a huge, exciting, powerful life… if you are wondering how you will pay the rent, trying to hide the scuffs on your three year old shoes, unhappily single and forty pounds overweight, *don't whatever you do, go for your biggest goal first.*

I don't say this simply because you could end up disappointed. Working on big goals up front can be far more dangerous than merely failing to achieve what you were looking for.

At worst, it leads to your manifesting *all your worst-case scenarios.*

Let me ask you a question: Have you ever tried to create a particular important goal using the Law of Attraction only to manifest the exact *opposite of what you asked for*? I certainly have.

For a long time, I had a habit of creating really quite horrifyingly opposite results to the ones I had been intending. Usually, this was nothing *overly* serious – a sudden bill would arrive when I had been trying to manifest money, I would try to manifest a weight loss and put on weight (four weeks at Weightwatchers and I gained every week!) These sorts of results happened enough times for me to become more than disillusioned with the process. I actually became *afraid* of it! I became afraid of working on goals at all, for fear of bringing bad things into my life.

As we have seen, by constantly focusing on it, asking for it, and so wanting it, it is possible to prevent a goal from manifesting. But why on earth would the *opposite* manifest?

It is really quite simple. When you think about wanting more money, you actually tend to end up thinking about your state of poverty. When you aim to lose weight, you end up focusing on how fat you look and feel. In trying to change these things, you end up spending even *more time thinking about things you do not want than you normally would*. Thinking about your dearest heart's desire just highlights how far away you are from your dream, showing up your unsatisfactory life in depressing detail, making you feel that sense of lack even more keenly. You basically end up focusing on exactly the opposite of what you are trying to manifest. So the Magic responds and gives you exactly what you think about.

There is yet another type of unwanted situation which can befall you when working on big goals too soon. This one can be even more heart-breaking than manifesting the opposite.

One of the most terrifying things that can happen to any new practitioner of Magic is what has been described by some as a 'snap-back'. This is the horrifying experience of having things go suddenly and drastically wrong, *just as you thought you had turned a corner.* The snap-back tends to happen when a fantastic, life-changing manifestation occurs. You may have apparently manifested the perfect mate, a huge sum of money, or a dream job. All seems well with the world. You have done it –

you have manifested something from your wildest dreams.

But then... it all comes crashing down. You find your new soul mate in bed with your best friend; a huge and unexpected bill wipes out all your new-found money; the company who offered you the dream job goes bust, just as you have given in notice at your old company.

Has something similarly frightening happened to you? Has it happened so many times that you have begun to fear the whole manifestation process? You should be afraid, because this turn of events is no coincidence. The snap-back happens when you have unsuspectingly carried out a perfect and momentary act of perfect Magic. You have cast the perfect spell, waved the magic wand Harry Potter-style and the object of your desires has appeared. But, as Spiderman says, with great power comes great responsibility. If you are not *ready* to receive the manifestation, *it will not stick around!* Let me repeat that in a different way: if you have worked a piece of Magic but have not worked sufficiently on *you*, on turning yourself into the person that can handle the manifestation, a person that *fits* that goal, **then you will lose it.**

This is why some lottery winners often lose all their money a couple of years after the initial win. It's because they don't have the rest of the life to match it. They don't have a millionaire mind-set, a millionaire way of doing things and their non-millionaire friends become greedy and resentful. So, the snap-back occurs, life reflects the person, not the desire, and the money is lost.

So, to recap this important point:

If you manifest a huge sum of money, but on a background of feeling unworthy, acting poor, dressing, acting, believing, thinking like a poor person, *you will lose all your money.*

If you manifest a perfect partner, but you don't feel attractive, feel unlovable and unworthy, if you have not allocated time and space in your life for such a person, *they will leave you.*

If you manifest any wonderful bit of good fortune, despite a background of worry, complaining, poor beliefs and negativity, *it will leave you!*

If you go in 'too high' with your initial manifestations, the rest of your person just won't be in agreement with your new-found fortune, and the snap-back will occur, reliably and spectacularly.

If *you* are not ready, you will lose it, *every* time.

The ironic thing is that the opposite is also true. This is why rich and 'fortunate' people are able to bounce back so quickly from misfortune. Their mind-set is so positive that little bits of misfortune will tend to be followed by an equal or greater bit of fortune. This is the main reason the rich get richer and the poor get poorer. 'Bad' things still happen to the most magical people, but because their background state is set to positivity, luck and fortune, these mishaps are nothing but minor blips in an otherwise perfect life.

I hope by now you are becoming convinced: if you are not *already* able to manifest at will and with ease, you should forget all about *thoughts become things* for now.

In fact, in the early days, I suggest *you don't work on particular desires or goals* **at all**, not even small ones.

You may reply: 'Forget about *thoughts become things* and *do not* work on specific goals? What sort of system is this? A useless one! What's the point?'

Let me make this clear: if you are setting out to manifest a particular thing, person or situation in your life, you had better be damned good at it. If not, chances are it *will* go spectacularly wrong. By going for your number one goal before you are ready to receive, you court complete disaster.

What's worse, every time you make a mistake, you will do immense harm to your belief in your own ability. And if you don't believe, you can't do Magic.

If you ever want to be really proficient in creating the life you desire, you must lay the preparation and *become* Magic before you can *do* Magic. Magic is not something separate from you; it is not something you *do*. Magic is something you *are*. So it is imperative you start out by getting *you* right, preparing and getting a sense of your own inner power, before moving on to manifesting *any* specific goals. Become Magic, and your life will change in the most amazing ways. You will avoid snap-backs and mistakes. The process of manifestation will become effortless and you truly will be able to make a life of joy and wonder.

This approach may be hard to swallow for someone who has been seduced by the lure of other Law of Attraction writers, by those who are *desperate* to change their lives, *now*. But notice that I did not say you could not begin changing your life immediately for the better. I only advise you not to work on particular goals yet.

It is perfectly possible to experience profound and wonderful changes in your life, by doing nothing other than following the preparation advice in this book. You may even find that having seen these results, you no longer feel the need to work on your goals at all, and would rather let life play out as one big game, full of surprises.

If you insist, you can fight to make your biggest goals manifest immediately and risk getting the same sorts of results as you have until now (or worse) ... or you can learn patience, work on yourself, let things take as long as they need, and watch your life begin to change *without effort* in miraculous and fantastical ways. Your choice.

The remainder of this book is dedicated to showing you how to start going about becoming a truly magical person. When you become proficient enough to move on to *Doing Magic*, and to start deliberate creation, you will find your manifestation attempts work smoothly, quickly, powerfully.

IMPORTANT NOTE

Before we move on, it is important to realize that not every snap-back is a true snap-back. When making big changes in your life, be prepared for a bit of a shake-up. Changes are afoot, and odd, drastic and unforeseen things are to be expected here. So, even if an apparent snap-back does befall you, refuse to see it as a bad thing. A snap-back can be seen as evidence that something is happening, something is changing, *fast*. So fast that you cannot keep up. So take snap-backs in your stride, recognize that they are evidence of your own magical power, and keep going. Every 'disaster' contains the seed of something wonderful and who knows whether that apparent disaster is a stepping stone to success?

How can you tell if it is a snap-back or a stepping stone to something more wonderful? ***You can't.***

So just choose to view them all as stepping stones. And remember, even a genuine snap-back is a sort of stepping stone in itself – leading you to a greater and better understanding of the process. Keep this sort of attitude up and before long they *will* all be stepping stones.

9 HOW TO MAKE IT WORK

Without adequate preparation, without *working on you,* your results are going to remain disappointing. You can ask until you are blue in the face, but if you continue to *ask* before having got *you* right, you might as well save your breath.

Let's look at an analogy: How do you run a marathon? It is really very straightforward: just keep your eye on the finish line, do not stop running, drink your electrolytes as you go, and remember to breathe. That is what marathon runners do. So that's what we all must do in order to run a marathon, yes?

Well, yes, this *is* true. This *is* what marathon runners do when running a marathon. So why would a newcomer to running find these simple instructions *so* difficult to stick to? It's because *they haven't worked on themselves.* The marathon runner doesn't just follow the instructions on how to run a race. They have to train for months and months beforehand. They have to prepare, physically, mentally and emotionally beforehand. They know there is a lot more to running than just putting one foot in front of the other. It is *exactly* the same with Magic.

I'm going to come clean: this book contains no instructions on how to do Mor ask for what you want. None!

Remember, this is a *course* in Magic. The reason I separated the two short books into separate volumes is not 'to make more money'. I would actually probably make more money if I published both books in one volume. No, I separated the parts so that you would be forced to read them, *one at a time and hopefully in the right order.*

This is part one *Becoming Magic.* It is not called *Doing Magic,* with good reason. It's not possible to *do* Magic *on* the world. You must become that which you want to be *first* and let the world follow in your tracks. This means no one can successfully, consistently and intentionally do Magic *until they have become Magic*. And here is the really exciting thing about this – you don't have to work hard to change the world. The only thing you have to change is *you* ... and watch the world follow.

What sort of person are you? What are your beliefs, what are your predominant thoughts? Are you generally happy, but often moody? Easily upset, a bit of a worrier. Work hard but unorganized. Are your thoughts a bit all-over-the place? Now look at your life. Is it full of things that make you worry? A bit unorganized? Are your results all-over-the-place? Your world faithfully and accurately reflects, not what you have put in an order for, not what you have correctly and clearly asked for, but *the person you are!*

Most of you even now, will skip straight to book two, *Doing Magic* and begin the asking phase of Magic, even though I have written this entire book telling you of the pitfalls of asking before you are ready. Don't be that person.

10 HOW TO PREPARE ADEQUATELY FOR ASKING

Pick a day to start your new life. It is a good idea to mark this out in some way, a ceremonial way. You may stage a little ritual of your own at home, write down a declaration on paper and sign in. Or you can make your declaration, semi-publicly to me by sending me an email of your declared intention to begin your new life.

Email genevievedavis@outlook.com

We have all heard this so many times it has almost become a cliché but you must take responsibility for your own life. And when I say take responsibility, I mean *really* take responsibility.

Do not pay lip service to this step. It is *essential.*

Whenever I am emailed with questions, almost all are along the lines of *I did this precise thing but nothing happened, why didn't it work? Or: I had this funny feeling and this happened, and then I thought this this and this, is it working? Or: I did what you said but I did not get my goal, I need some help.* And my answer to all of these sorts of questions?

I cannot do this for you.

This is one fact that you need to burn into your brain – *I cannot do this for you!* Much of learning how to do Magic is about *discovering, feeling, noticing, noting, realizing, sensing, coming to know,* and very little about being *told.* The answer to almost all of your questions will come, not from being told a new piece of information, but from an experience of your own, a realization you have, seeing the truth of something, watching something work *in your own life.*

There is a reason that these books are so short, and it is *not* because I have run out of things to say! These books are short because as soon as possible you need to stop reading and start experiencing the truth of these words for yourself.

Mastering Magic is about personal experience and experimentation, about feeling things for yourself, about getting 'a sense' of what I am saying. No matter how many times I tell you something, or in whatever language I put it, until you have experienced it for yourself, my words will mean squat.

Notice, learn, record

If you spend your weekends sitting in pajamas, watching daytime television, eating junk food and wishing the phone would ring, and wondering 'where all the good men have gone', don't be surprised when you don't get the results you want.

If you do a visualization or ritual, set an intention and then get angry when it doesn't manifest immediately, or blame the writer of the book or the creator of the system, don't be surprised that you didn't get the results you wanted.

If you think that my saying 'I cannot do this for you' is just a way of absolving myself of my own duties to you then don't be surprised when you don't get the results you want.

Understand that I am less of a teacher and more of a signpost. It is totally up to you to take the steps. It is totally up to you to make this work. A bad workman blames his tools. A bad student blames her teacher. A good student of Magic blames no one, learns from the experience, and moves on.

STOP COMPLAINING, FULL STOP

Complaining, worrying and moaning are endemic in almost every advanced society in the world. I have travelled all around this big world, and visited people from all backgrounds and all cultures. Complaining and focusing on the negative at the expense of the positive is prevalent in every society. However, I have also noticed something else: there is a *very* clear correlation between those who are very happy and an almost non-existent level of complaining. It bemuses me that there has never been any real scientific research done into this correlation.

Those who complain a lot, generally have lives that are poorer in all ways than those who do not complain. Those who do not complain, generally have fuller, richer and happier lives. And, I am *not* talking of material riches here. Money is only one small part of what it means to have wealth.

'That's obvious!' you reply. 'Those with a lot *have* nothing to complain about. If you knew what I had to contend with, you'd know why I complain!'

I want you to consider the possibility that this way of interpreting things is completely backwards. I want you to accept on faith for now, (and eventually come to believe completely) that some people *have* a lot precisely because they *don't* complain.

Conversely, it is complaining that keeps you in a state of wanting. You can faithfully follow the steps of a manifestation procedure, but if you are walking around in a terrible mood, complaining about everything on earth, bemoaning your lot in life, angry and jealous about why your life didn't turn out the way you wanted, nothing will ever turn out well for you.

Complaining just invites more into your life to complain about because complaining means wanting things to be different.

And wanting is the opposite of having.

So, the very first phase in the magical process is to clear away the dross, the negativity, the complaining, the moaning, the worrying, the seeing everything in a bad light, the thinking of the worst, the telling of a bleak and bitter story of life. Kick your complaining addiction. Why addiction? Because complaining is a difficult habit to break and it will take a good deal of effort for you to eradicate it from your life.

Once the habit is kicked, and you have experienced life from this peaceful new place, you will come to realize and feel the effect that complaining has on you, mentally and physically. It will no longer feel 'right' to complain and you will feel uncomfortable indulging it.

When I now meet a person who complains a lot, it physically pains me. I feel a sinking sensation, my anxiety raises and I begin to feel really, really uncomfortable. In this situation, I usually do my best to extricate myself from that person and their energy as soon as possible.

You have probably heard the virtues of positive thinking. But rather than trying to think positively, it is much easier and more effective when starting out simply to *stop thinking negatively.*

So stop complaining. No exceptions. This does not mean lying down and taking whatever life throws at you like some sort of doormat. Neither does it mean eating a cold meal in a restaurant because you feel you mustn't complain. Complaints to a specific and relevant person in order to bring about a change of affairs are obviously permitted. What *is not* allowed is complaining for the sake of complaining – talking in a negative way about something for fun, to gossip about someone in a derogatory way, to pass the time of day, or worse, to make you feel better, more important or as a way of connecting with another negative person.

Compare: *My food is cold, please bring me a fresh meal.*

With: *I had the worst meal ever last night. The food was stone cold. I am never going back to that place. What a waste of money. It's hard enough coping on my salary without having this sort of thing happen. But that's my life. Nothing good ever happens to me.*

The instruction to stop complaining *includes* bemoaning the state of the world, society, the government and 'just how bad things are these days'. I also suggest you stop reading newspapers, watching the news, or reading gossip magazines. Gossip magazines are legalized bullying. They engender spite, resentment, jealously and represent some of the vilest and basest of human tendencies. And if you think it is ok to bully, lie and gossip about celebrities because they are rich, I suggest to work quickly to change that destructive belief – it isn't helping you.

The world is addicted to negativity and the media is largely responsible for this. Most people's lives actually run fairly smoothly and things tend to turn out for the best. But you would think we were on the brink of Armageddon, from all the messages of terror in the news.

Many people are shocked, even disgusted that I refuse to read newspapers. 'But how will you know what is going on in the world,' they ask.

I have many, many detailed arguments about why I don't read newspapers. For now, I just want you to recognize that newspapers tell almost exclusively bad news. Most of them twist the truth to the extent that only lies are told (even by the more 'respectable' papers). And even if a story is 100% true, it is almost certainly a negative or fear-mongering story.

If you want to change the world, then go and change it. Do something, act. Or better still, become magically powerful and realize just how much good you can do from this new place. But don't ever complain about the state of the world, or anything else, unless you are directly working to change it. Sharing a Facebook status about the latest government betrayal does *nothing* to change that injustice. All it does is momentarily make you feel important, while at the same time winding you up, lowering your energy and taking you one step further away from your true magical power.

Don't move on until you are in agreement with me on this. Trying to consciously manifest important goals before you have tackled your own background levels of negativity is worthless.

PRACTISE GRATITUDE

Go to an art shop or bookshop and buy a small notebook, one that will fit in your handbag, briefcase, rucksack or pocket. Try to buy something of quality, one that looks and feels of good quality. Paperblanks are a brand which make some beautiful little hardback books or, you can buy a little Moleskin or similar.

Every morning you will take one page, put the date at the top and write down three things for which you are grateful, in that moment. In the evening, before bed, write down another three.

You can also jot down various times in the day when something strikes you. It could be something tiny *I am grateful that I got a seat on the bus this morning. I am grateful that Susan had that nice chat with me. I am grateful that my sandwich tasted so good today.* Or, they can be much more profound and important things *I am so grateful that I am so fit and healthy. I am so grateful for my wonderful husband. I am so grateful to have two healthy children. I am so grateful that I am becoming proficient in Magic.*

Try to think of a different set every day. And when you do this, actually try and *feel* the sense of gratitude.

If 'gratitude' does not mean a great deal to you, then choose whatever words ring better with you. Rather than a 'gratitude journal', consider an 'I am so happy' journal or a 'how wonderful!' journal. For example, *how wonderful that I got a seat on the bus, I'm so happy that Susan had a nice chat with me.* Or, you could mix it up. You could write down things you are grateful for, happy about or just whatever makes you feel good. The point is not to get the words right, the point is to change your focus to all the good that is in your life. Your energy will rise automatically and naturally just by this one move.

Don't just write down the words, *feel it.* Do not write down things that you feel you ought to be grateful for, but aren't. This process needs genuinely to evoke the emotion of gratitude, happiness or wonder. And don't ever, *ever* miss this out because you cannot think of anything positive to say, or because you had a bad day. If you cannot think of something *think harder!* There is always something good you can find to focus on.

At first, it will just feel like you are going through the motions. But by doing this process repeatedly, you will gain momentum quickly. Remember, the world is but a reflection of you.

A person who notices a lot of good in their life, *has a lot of good in their life.* A person who is grateful a lot, *has a lot to be grateful for.* It works that way around. Look at the world and smile, and it will smile back at you.

11 NOTICE THE GROWTH OF YOUR OWN MAGICAL ABILITY

Rather than mere thoughts, it is your deeply held beliefs which have the greatest effect on your life. Your beliefs will inform your thoughts, produce feelings and actions based on those beliefs. So it is *essential* that you begin to believe in your own magical power. You need to believe in your own power, *really* believe it; not just wishfully think it. Not just say 'I believe in myself' in some sort of self-help sound bite-type way, while inside part of you is disagreeing.

At present, you may feel so out of control that you don't even know *how* it would feel to be powerful. So how do you create a belief in your own inherent magical power from a place of apparent powerlessness? *Slowly!*

This is yet another reason for not working on goals too quickly. Any failure in achieving a particular goal will only dent your belief; we cannot risk that. But, every success, no matter how small, will grow your belief in your own ability. Little tiny successes all build into a wonderful strong belief.

'But isn't it best to learn from mistakes?'

Sometimes, yes. But with Magic because the results are often spectacularly bad at first, you *never get the chance to learn from them.* Most people never move past this stage. Poor or frightening results, or a snap-back come along to crush that fresh new belief, you give up, and move on to the next thing, book, or approach.

But by starting small, by doing nothing other than making some small changes in yourself, you will see modest but *immediate and solid* results. From there you can build your belief and your power, slowly yes, but *strongly and surely.* All the time, your power, belief and confidence will be growing. Your Magic will begin showing itself more often and before long, you will no longer need proof. You will know it.

Slowly, steadily, surely, your belief in your own magical power will grow. And when belief in your own magical power grows, *your magical power grows!* The stronger your belief in your own power, the greater your magical ability.

Having worked hard for a few days (preferably weeks) to eradicate the bulk of your negativity, you start noticing the effect of doing this. Notice, accept and believe that small changes in *you* do indeed bring about a positive change in the people, events and situations around you.

See the world, not as a separate realm over which you have greater or lesser effect, but as a mirror, reflecting not just your thoughts, but *you.*

Notice that when you smile, the world smiles back at you, in every way. Expecting the world to change, without changing *you* is like looking into a mirror and expecting the reflection to smile first. The world simply will never change, until you change.

Begin to realize that your experience of life is nothing but a reflection of the person you are.

Are you beginning to notice the way that little things seem to be turning out for the best?

Have you noticed that things generally do not turn out as badly as you perhaps expected? Have any small bits of good fortune started to come your way?

Are you generally feeling more positive, optimistic, happier, lighter?

This is the first point at which you may actually start to feel the first inkling that you have an inner power that can affect the circumstances and world around you.

This is a crucial point.

It is at this point that things can go one of two ways: The wrong way to go is to start *explaining away* your little bits of good fortune as fluke or coincidence.

The right way to go is to go too far in the other direction, describing *everything* that happens in terms of your own power. See every tiny innocuously fortuitous event as part of the same picture, as evidence of your effect on the world. Even apparently 'bad' things can be viewed merely as necessary stepping stones on the way to something wonderful.

You will then automatically begin looking for more instances of this new found ability to affect the world. Everything that happens will serve to increase your belief, and you will be well on your way to becoming truly Magic and adept at creating your own life.

Want to be all powerful, capable of great Magic? Then just decide to be so. Having trouble with holding that belief immediately? Then start looking for evidence that it is true. If you look for little bits of evidence, *you will find them.*

You see, it really doesn't matter how you get to that belief. It doesn't matter how unlikely or flimsy the evidence. Just choose to interpret everything in the way that supports your belief.

Becoming Magic is not about learning something new. It is about turning your focus inwards and noticing what was already there.

It has *always* been the case that your life reflects your beliefs, but perhaps you have never noticed it until now.

By coming to see the actual occasions in your own life where this is happening, you become *aware* of the power that was always there. You need to really see for yourself the *actual* effect of your *actual* efforts. You need to see irrefutable evidence *with your own eyes.*

Remember, you are *highly* unlikely to get to this sort of strong belief in your own power when trying to manifest big goals up front. The chances of things going wrong are just too great. So, before you think of moving on to *asking* you must be fully prepared.

Pick a day to make your declaration, and then commit to the following vital preparations.

1. Take responsibility for your life

2. Stop complaining/moaning/criticizing

3. Keep a gratitude journal

BE AWARE OF THE RESULTS

Do this for *at least* two weeks or until you begin to notice the effect this is having on your outlook, your mood and on your life circumstances. If you prefer, you can keep this up for 30-60 days, by which time it will have become a habit that has transformed your life in incredible ways.

12 WHEN TO MOVE ON TO BOOK TWO: *DOING MAGIC*

I strongly suggest that you move on to book two when the following conditions have been met.

1. Complaining and being negative has begun to feel uncomfortable

2. You have an underlying feeling of things having 'picked up' or that you feel optimistic and excited about the future.

3. You have actually begun to notice that your life has started to reflect your new positive outlook.

4. You are beginning to get an *inkling* of your own power and ability.

If you are feeling impatient, do not quite agree with what I have said about negativity, or are really not sure if you have noticed *anything* at all, *go back. You are not ready.*

When 1 - 4 are true, you are ready to move on to the next part of the course. In *Doing Magic* you will learn the very steps that took me from miserable poverty, crippling debt, living in a shoddy flat in a bad part of town, just divorced and single, few friends and an almost constant deep depression to where I am now. I now live life like one big, fun game. My life feels like Christmas and the best birthday party I have ever had, *every day.* It is like being in love, feeling more safe, more secure, more 'at one with the world' than I ever knew was possible. I didn't realize a life like this was available to me, especially considering how things had turned out in the first 40 years of my life. *This is the sort of life that is waiting for you too!*

BY THE SAME AUTHOR

Becoming Rich: A Method for
Manifesting Exceptional Wealth

Now in paperback

27821680R00054

Printed in Great Britain
by Amazon